Subhas Chandra Bose

The 'Passionate Patriot'

Reeta Dutta Gupta

Rupa . Co

In loving memory of Brokaku—Late Sachin Chandra Dutta Gupta
—a Calcuttan of the first order

Published in 2005 by

Rupa . Co

7/16, Ansari Road, Daryaganj
New Delhi 110 002

Sales Centres:
Allahabad Bangalore Chandigarh Chennai
Hyderabad Jaipur Kathmandu
Kolkata Mumbai Pune

Cover & Book Design by
Arrt Creations
45 Nehru Apts, Kalkaji
New Delhi 110 019

Printed in India by
International Print-O-Pac Ltd.
B204, B205, B206, Okhala Industrial Area-I
New Delhi-20

CONTENTS

Chapter One

The 'Passionate Patriot'

At the age of five, when the child Subhas was told that he would soon be sent to school, he was overjoyed. Recalling that day, he wrote in his book, *An Indian Pilgrim: An Unfinished Autobiography*:

'It was to be a red letter day for me. At long last I was going to join the grown-up respectable folks . . . Two uncles of about the same age as myself were also to be admitted along with myself. When we were all ready, we began to run towards the carriage, which was to take us to school. Just then, as ill-luck would have it, I slipped and fell. I was hurt and, with a bandage round my head, I was ordered to bed. The rumbling of the carriage wheels grew fainter in the distance. The lucky ones had gone, but there I lay with darkness staring me in the face and my fond hopes dashed to the ground.'

Years later, when the Second World War broke out, Bose hoped for his final red-letter day, when he would march to Delhi with his soldiers to deliver freedom to his countrymen and women. Then at long last, he would rejoin the elder nationalists at home with whom he had parted ways when he escaped to Germany in 1941, to seek the support of the Axis powers in order to oust the British from Indian soil. But as ill-luck would have it, the battle was lost. And just two years before Independence, on 23 August 1945, Bose succumbed to the ultimate darkness of death—with a severely burnt body swathed in bandages, following the plane crash in Taiwan, in which he was travelling.

Janaki Nath Bose and family, 1905; Subhas Bose (standing, extreme right)

Though vanquished by fate like a tragic hero, Subhas Chandra Bose's life was filled with acts of extraordinary courage and conviction. Born on Saturday, 23 January 1897, in a small town in Orissa, the story of his life is a heroic saga of self-sacrifice for the cause of India's freedom.

'Never for a moment falter in your faith in India's destiny. There is no power on earth that can keep India enslaved. India shall be free and before long,' he had stated. And throughout his life, he had one dream, one passion, and one sole purpose—to free his country from the shackles of British colonialism. Selflessly, he dedicated his entire life to this task, undertaking untold hardships and daring to do things that can only be described as most daunting. He was the 'prince among patriots', as Mahatma Gandhi acknowledged, despite his sharp ideological differences with the man. 'India, our motherland' was for Bose 'God's beloved land,' at whose altar he finally laid down his life.

Bose as a teenager

The Bose family descended from the Boses of Mahinagar, a village about 22 km to the south of Calcutta (now Kolkata). Some of his ancestors rose to eminence in the royal court of Bengal, receiving titles and property grants. Later, one of the Boses moved to the adjoining village of Kodalia. The name of the village was derived from *kodal*, meaning spade, that was used to dig a water tank at the initiative of an ancestor with a zeal for social reform. Subhas Chandra Bose's father, Janakinath Bose (1860-1934), was born in this village. After passing the Matriculation

Father Janakinath Bose

Examination from Calcutta, he went to Cuttack—then a small town in pre-independent Bengal Presidency, which included Bihar, Orissa and Chhota Nagpur—and did his graduation from Ravenshaw College. Later, he took his Bachelor of Law Examination from the Metropolitan Institution, Calcutta, founded by the scholar and social reformer Ishwar Chandra Vidyasagar. After joining the Bar in 1885, he soon made his mark in the legal profession, becoming the government pleader and prosecutor in 1905, and a member of the Bengal Legislative Council in 1912. Addressed as 'Janakinath Sahib' for his anglicised tastes and habits, he however, often returned to his village—to his roots, and is said to have financially helped with the education of needy boys and provided his village with a library and a dispensary. In 1930, when Mahatma Gandhi launched the Civil Disobedience Movement, Janakinath renounced the title of *Rai Bahadur* that the British Government had given him for his loyalty to the Raj.

Mother Prabhabati Bose

Bose's father Janakinath and mother Prabhabati (b. 1869)—she belonged to the family of the Duttas of Hatkhola of north Calcutta—were married in 1880 at the age of twenty and eleven, respectively. Subhas Bose was the sixth son and the ninth child of his parents.

Bose began his primary education at the Protestant European School run by the Baptist Mission in Cuttack in 1902 at the age of five. There, he writes, '. . . We had to train our ears to "Do, Rey, Me, Fa," and not to "Sa, Rey, Ga, Ma".' He left this school to join Ravenshaw Collegiate School, Cuttack, in 1909, at the age of twelve. The school principal was Babu Benimadhab Das, a man who left an abiding impression on his youthful mind. 'Up till then I had never experienced what it was to respect a man. But for me, to see Beni Madhav Das was to adore him. I was not old enough then to realise what it was that I adored. I could only feel that here was a man who was not an ordinary teacher, who stood apart from, and above, the rest of his tribe,' Bose wrote in his unfinished autobiography. Das aroused in the boy moral and spiritual values and taught him to 'love nature and be inspired by her.' Here Bose was also introduced to Indian traditions and he learnt Bengali, his mother tongue, as well as Sanskrit, the two subjects that were not offered at the Europeanised primary school. Later Bose recalled: 'For weeks and months the Bengali lessons would give me the creeps. But for the time being, however acute the mental torture, there was nothing I could do but put up with the humiliation and secretly resolved to make good. Slowly and steadily I began to gain ground and at the annual examination I had the satisfaction of getting the highest marks in that subject.'

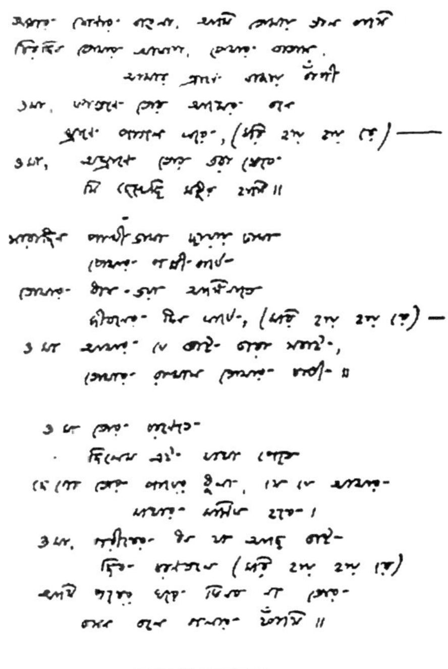

Bose's handwritten Bengali version of Rabindranath Tagore's song Amar Sonar Bangla *– later adopted as the national anthem of Bangladesh*

A bright and diligent student throughout his educational career, Bose however, 'did not take kindly to sports and only the drill lessons interested me,' he wrote. He passed the Matriculation Examination in 1913 with flying colours, securing the second position. After this he, like his brothers, was 'packed off to Calcutta' at the age of sixteen-and-a-half years to join the city's premier higher education institute, the Presidency College. Writing about his impression of the city of Calcutta, which he had been visiting since his infancy and where his family came to set up its establishment at Elgin Road, Bose described it as a 'great city' that 'intrigued me, bewildered me beyond measure. I had loved to roam about its wide streets and among its gardens and museums and I had felt that one could not see enough of it. It was like a leviathan which one could look at from outside and go on admiring. But this time I came to settle down there and to mix with its inner life.'

Such was the love that Bose, like all Calcuttans, came to feel for the city that, as Anthony Read and David Fisher wrote in their book, *The Proudest Day: India's Long Road to Independence*, he once saved it from being

Ramakrishna Paramahansa – guru of Swami Vivekananda

bombed by the Japanese during the Second World War. When Bose went to the Andamans in 1943 as the chief of the Indian National Army, he '. . . did manage to achieve one practical result at that time: getting wind of a proposed air raid on Calcutta, he convinced the Japanese that the political consequences of bombing the city would far outweigh any temporary military advantage, and he managed to persuade them to abandon the plan.'

Swami Vivekananda

After passing his Intermediate Examination in first division, in 1915 at the age of eighteen Bose studied philosophy with honours, a subject that had always attracted him. Earlier, when he was barely fifteen, he became deeply interested in the teachings of Swami Vivekananda and then 'turned gradually to his master, *Ramakrishna* Paramahansa.' Bose came across the works of Swami Vivekananda in a relative's house next door. He recalled later: 'I had hardly turned over a few pages when I realised that here was something which I had been looking for . . . For days, weeks, months I poured over his works. His letters as well as his speeches from Colombo and Almora, replete as they were with practical advice to his countrymen, inspired me most. From this study I emerged with a vivid idea of the essence of his teachings . . . the service of humanity included, of course, the service of one's country.'

During this period of his life, Bose experienced an inner restlessness, a psychic angst that made him turn to spirituality. He became deeply interested in yoga and sadhus and along with a group of friends, he often took long walks and excursions, which gave them 'greater

Even after 50 years of independence, real India is one where poverty and illiteracy stalk the land

opportunities for meeting and discussion.' His parents did not approve of this obsession and he writes in his autobiography, 'I was questioned, warned in a friendly manner, and ultimately rebuked. I was rapidly changing and was no longer the goody-goody boy afraid of displeasing his parents. I had a new ideal before me now which had inflamed my soul—to effect my own salvation and to serve humanity by abandoning all worldly desires and breaking away from all undue restraints. I no longer recited Sanskrit verses inculcating obedience to one's parents; on the contrary, I took to verses which preached defiance.' And once during the summer vacation of 1914, the young adult left home quietly with a friend without his parent's knowledge to wander in search of a guru, who, he hoped, would show him the path to truth. However, 'this tour which lasted nearly two months brought us in touch not only with a number of holy men, but also with some of the patent shortcomings of the Hindu society, and I returned home a wiser man, having lost much of my admiration for ascetics.' he wrote.

From an early age, Bose felt the desire to serve the less privileged. And he became increasingly conscious of the injustices of the social system, the chasm that existed between the haves and have-nots, and frequently undertook social service like collecting relief funds for the victims of flood or famine. Once, while nursing patients with a group of friends during a cholera epidemic, when on a vacation in Cuttack at the end of his first year in college, he was deeply touched by the depressive picture of the real India. He wrote, 'In those days cholera was regarded as a fatal disease and it was not easy to get people to attend cholera patients. Our party was absolutely fearless in that respect . . . a week's experience opened a new world before my eyes and unfolded a picture of real India, the India of the villages—where poverty stalks over the land, men die like flies and illiteracy is the prevailing order.'

Writes Leonard A Gordon, the biographer of Subhas Bose and his brother, Sarat Bose, in his acclaimed book *Brothers Against The Raj*: 'From his early years Subhas displayed a nurturing side to his personality. He took a great interest in raising plants and working in the garden when other boys were at play. As he entered his teens, he began to find situations in which he had to nurse others, often poor people who were generally neglected in their distress.' And Bose himself wrote, 'Gardening I found absorbingly interesting. It served, among other things, to open my eyes to the beauties of nature.'

During his undergraduate days, Bose joined an active group of students with revolutionary beliefs. British India was then the hotbed of racial discrimination and eventually, the fiery young Bose was drawn into its politics. An incident in his college led to an open confrontation with the college authorities. When E F Oaten, an English professor, manhandled a group of students for allegedly causing a disturbance, the students responded by going on a strike—something that was simply unheard of in those colonial times. Later, the strike was withdrawn and the dispute settled, but a fine was slapped on the disgruntled students. But then, the very next month, a similar incident involving the same professor occurred once again. This time the students

Bose took a great interest in raising plants and working in the garden

took the law in their hands and beat him up. Bose was named in the incident and he was rusticated from college and debarred from studying further at the University. The Principal bellowed, 'Bose, you are the most troublesome man in the College. I suspend you.' Bose replied, 'Thank you,' and returned home, taking a train to Cuttack.

The year was 1916. Bose later recorded, 'Lying on the bunk in the train at night I reviewed the events of the last few months. My educational career was at an end, and my future was dark and uncertain. But I was not sorry—there was not a trace of regret in my mind for what I had done. I had rather a feeling of supreme satisfaction, of joy that I had done the right thing, that I had stood up for our honour and self-respect and had sacrificed myself for a noble cause. After all, what is life without renunciation, I told myself. And I went to sleep. Little did I then realise the inner significance of the tragic event of 1916. My Principal had expelled me, but he had made my future career.'

Young Bose (standing) on the eve of his departure for Cambridge, England, with his father, Janakinath Bose

In 1917, after a year, Bose returned to Calcutta seeking re-admission to an institute to complete his studies. He was able to join the Scottish Church College for the honours course in philosophy. As Bose had always been keen on gaining military training (he had tried unsuccessfully earlier to join the 49th Bengal Regiment, but was disqualified because of poor vision), he now joined the university unit of the India Defence Force or Territorial Army. He was convinced that, 'Political freedom was indivisible and what is more, a liberated nation must have military strength to preserve its independence.'

Group photograph of India Defence Force, Calcutta University, 1917

Bose took his BA degree with a first class in 1919 and though he now wanted to study experimental psychology for his MA Examination, his father had other plans for him. He wished to send his son to England to take the open competitive examination to join the prestigious Indian Civil Service (ICS). He recalled, 'I only remember hearing in talks within the family circle that the highest position one could get to was the Indian Civil Services.'

On 15 September 1919, Bose sailed for England, even though he himself was doubtful of successfully passing the highly competitive ICS examination. But once in England, he worked diligently as ever, having just nine months to prepare for the examination. He also enrolled for Mental and Moral Sciences Tripos at Cambridge, while his extra-curricular activities involved participation in Indian Majlis and the Union Society. And though Bose himself was not sure of clearing the ICS examination, he came fourth in the merit list, and was selected for the cream Service in 1920. But far from rejoicing in his success, he now became torn by a dilemma, 'What should I do with the job? Was I going to give the go-by to all my dreams and aspirations, and settle down to a comfortable life? . . . But . . . I had certain ideals, which I wanted to live up to. It was therefore quite impossible for me to go into the Service unless I could make a clean sweep of my past life.'

Bose debated within himself on this difficult issue and he penned long letters to his elder brother, Sarat, with whom he remained very close all his life, telling him how difficult it was for him to resolve the conflict in his mind between his ideals and social and financial responsibilities. Finally, at the risk of hurting his family members, his parents in particular, Bose wrote to his brother conveying his decision not to serve under the British Government, which he despised, and instead pursue his dreams. 'I am sure many of our relatives will howl when they hear of such a rash and dangerous proposal . . . But I do not care for their opinions, their cheers or their taunts,' he wrote and wondered in a letter to his brother Sarat, 'The Civil Service can bring one all kinds of worldly comfort but are not these acquisitions made at the expense of one's soul?'

The Bose brothers: Subhas and Sarat, 1937

Before finally withdrawing his nomination from the ICS, Bose debated as to the purpose of his life. Writing to Sarat, he wondered, 'If I give up the service, I shall not be in want of work to keep my hands full. Teaching, social service, cooperative credit work, journalism, village organisation work, these are so many things to keep thousands of energetic young men busy. Personally, I should like to take up teaching and journalism at present. The National College and the new paper *Swaraj* will afford plenty of scope for my activity.'

Bose took seven long months to make up his mind before he was convinced that it was not power, comfort and honour that he wanted, instead he was ready to accept hardship, poverty and suffering in order to serve his beloved country. He resigned from the ICS, refusing to wear 'the emblem of servitude.' And he was aware that '. . . in the whole history of British India, not one Indian has voluntarily given up the Civil Service with a patriotic motive.' Therefore, he urged, 'It is time that members of the highest service in India should set an example to members of the other services. If the members of the services withdraw their allegiance or even show a desire to do so—then only will the bureaucratic machine collapse.'

On 22 April 1921, writing to the Secretary of State for India, E S Montague, Bose withdrew his name from the list of probationers selected for the prestigious Service. Expectedly, not a few were taken aback by this bold and totally selfless decision. And as Bose himself wrote to his brother, 'I know how many hearts I have grieved, how many superiors of mine I have disobeyed but on the eve of this hazardous undertaking, my only prayer is—may it be for the good of our dear country.' And it was a great relief for him when he learnt that his mother too stood for the ideals of Mahatma Gandhi.

Having made the most crucial decision in his life, Bose, a man of destiny, sailed back to India in July 1921. Writes Leonard Gordon, 'This was the third of Subhas's youthful rebellions, the first, running away from home in search of a guru, the second, the attack on Professor Oaten and its consequences. In the second, he attacked the authority of a professor and of the educational hierarchy of the Raj in Bengal. Here he was rejecting a position in the elite service of the Raj, against the best advice and hopes of his father. But there was some ambivalence in all this. He wanted the authorities, including the British officials, to recognise his accomplishments, but he also wanted to put their prizes aside and follow his inner voice.'

'Azad Hind'

Chapter Two

In a 'Different Boat'

Having turned down the appointment to the high-profile Indian Civil Service at the age of twenty-three, Subhas Chandra Bose left England for India, then in the midst of an intense nationalist ardour following Mahatma Gandhi's nationwide call for non-cooperation in 1920. And the first man Bose went to meet at Mani Bhawan, the very afternoon he reached Bombay, was Gandhi.

However, Bose, the fiery young man with a 'revolutionary' bent of mind was 'disappointed' with the talks. Maybe as is said, he could not fully comprehend Gandhi, a man who had pinned his faith in non-violence. And over the years 'a certain coolness between the two men' developed, which was to result in a rift in 1939. Writes B R Nanda in *The Making of a Nation: India's Road to Freedom*, 'It is clear from Bose's own account of the interview that it was an unmitigated disaster; he was never able to develop empathy with Gandhi during the next twenty years; his attitude was to remain usually clinical, often critical, and occasionally antipathetic.'

But though Gandhi and Bose were to 'sail in different boats,' subscribing to opposing ideologies, Bose nonetheless held Gandhi in high esteem and for Gandhi, Bose was like a 'son'— only a very difficult one! After his stormy re-election as Congress President for the second time, Bose confessed, '. . . it will always be my aim and object to try and win his confidence for the simple reason that it will be a tragic thing for me if I succeed in winning the confidence of other people but fail to win the confidence of India's greatest man.'

From Bombay, Bose returned to Calcutta and acting on Gandhi's advice, he met Deshbandhu Chittaranjan Das, the Congress Working Committee member and the leader of Gandhi's Non-cooperation Movement in Bengal. Over the years C R Das and Bose developed a warm relationship. For young Bose, Das was his mentor and his wife, Basanti Das, his trusted and loved confidant. Das was impressed by the good-looking youth, his accomplishment and his self-sacrifice in turning down an ICS position, for which most young men

Deshbandhu Chittaranjan Das, the leader of Gandhi's Non-cooperation Movement in Bengal

hankered. He readily introduced Bose to the political scenario of the province, to its Youth Movement and the Trade Union Movement and assigned him important responsibilities.

Shortly afterwards, Bose became the Principal of the Bengal National College, one of the 800 schools and colleges set up throughout the country to replace government institutions boycotted during the Non-cooperation Movement. Bose also helped with the management of the nationalist weekly *Banglar Katha* (1921), *Atma Sakti* (1922) and the English-language daily *Forward* (1923). In 1923, he was elected President of the All Bengal Youth League and by the end of the year, became General Secretary of the Bengal Provincial Congress Committee, which he headed as the President towards the end of 1927. Bose also continued with social work through the Bhowanipore Sevak Samity. And throughout these years, he worked alongside Das with his characteristic single-minded determination and passionate enthusiasm, organising nationalist activities which in a short time made him the 'pet hate' of the British Government.

In December 1921, both Bose and Das were arrested when widescale arrests were made in Bengal to repress the Nationalist Movement, and the two were sent to Calcutta's Alipore Jail, where they spent eight months together. During this time the political fervour resulting from Gandhi's Satyagraha or non-cooperation and the boycott of all government offices, legislatures, educational institutes and law courts was at its peak. But in early 1922, villagers set fire to a police station killing some policemen in retaliation to a police firing in a small town of Chauri Chaura in the United Provinces. The Mahatma immediately withdrew the Non-cooperation Movement, as then it went against his principle of eschewing any form of violence. Both Das and Bose, who were then in prison, expressed their deep disappointment.

Shortly, by the end of 1922, following the suspension of the Non-Cooperation Movement, Das put forward a new plan of non-cooperation by calling for participation in provincial elections and then opposing the government from within the legislative body. However, this plan was defeated by those called the 'no-changers', who insisted on keeping out of legislatures. And when Motilal Nehru formed the Congressmen's Swaraj Party, Das, after resigning as the Congress President, joined the Swaraj Party along with Bose. In 1924, the Swarajists won the Calcutta Municipal Corporation election and Das became the first mayor of Calcutta, and Bose was appointed the Chief Executive Officer. Writes Sisir Kumar Bose in his biography *Netaji Subhas Chandra Bose*: 'For the first time, Khadi became the official uniform of civic employees and many streets and parks named after Britishers were re-named after India's greatest men. . . . Within a few months, Subhas was able to give a new orientation and momentum to the administration of the Corporation. The practice of giving civic receptions to British dignitaries was given up and instead the same was given to nationalist leaders when they visited the city . . . Subhas Chandra accepted half his salary as the Chief Executive and gave the other half to charity.'

In October 1924, Bose was arrested once again and from then on he was to be taken into custody eleven times, till he made his escape to Germany in 1940. From within prison walls, Bose continued to perform his official duties, but after a few months, he was put on a ship to Burma, where he was kept in lock-up in Mandalay. In 1925, when C R Das passed away, Bose suffered a great

Subhas Bose with Motilal Nehru (centre), the founder of Congressmen's Swaraj Party

loss. By the middle of 1927, Bose's health began to break down under the terrible conditions of Burmese prison life, and ill-health continued to plague him as he was jailed time and again. At last, he was set free after three long years.

In 1928, at the Calcutta summit of the Congress, Bose took charge of the Bengal Volunteer Corps for the training of youth along semi-military lines. He became its General Officer in Command. The Bengal Volunteer Corps practised military discipline with the members wearing military uniform. The Corps consisted of various divisions including a motorcycle unit, a cavalry unit and a Women's Corps. As Sisir Kumar Bose says, '. . . Subhas Chandra, thus, introduced a new element in the National Movement, viz., military discipline among national workers. What was in 1928 merely a vision came true in practical shape and form on the battlefields of South-east Asia during World War II.'

Described as a 'revolutionary' who represented the youth and the leftist forces in the National Movement like Jawaharlal Nehru, Bose wanted India to be 'an independent federal republic,' and not become a nation with a 'dominion status' (like Canada and Australia) within the British Empire. Writes Sugata Bose, professor of history, 'His demand at the Calcutta Congress of 1928 that "complete independence" instead of "dominion status" should be the goal of Indian nationalists was a sign that he was a step ahead of his contemporaries. He repeatedly spoke on behalf of the rights of three large communities—women, depressed classes and labouring masses.'

Congressmen had so far asked for dominion status, and it was only by the end of 1929 at the historic Lahore Congress with Jawaharlal Nehru as the President, that Gandhi supported the resolution for *Purna Swaraj*—complete independence. In January 1930, the Congress Working Committee declared 26 January to be observed as Independence Day throughout the country. On this day, for the first time, the tricolour flag was unfurled. And Bose went a step ahead, passing a resolution calling for a parallel government.

By 1929, the Indian Nationalist Movement took a revolutionary turn. Earlier in 1927 the British Government under Viceroy Lord Irwin had set up the Simon Commission to review the Indian situation and make further recommendations, but not a single Indian was represented on it. The nationalist leaders sharply condemned the Commission and when Sir John Simon arrived in India, he was greeted with slogans asking him to go back, which was accompanied by an outburst of hartals and boycott of British goods. During these protests, Lala Lajpat Rai, the noted Congressman from Punjab, was lathi-charged, resulting in his death from injuries. In vengeance, a British officer was assassinated for the assault.

Black flag processions everywhere greeted members of the Simon Commission

Other revolutionary acts also caught the nation's attention during this time. In 1929, a bomb was hurled in the Assembly Chamber in Delhi by Batukeshwar Dutt and Bhagat Singh, the leader of the Nawjawan Bharat Sabha, a youth organisation in the Punjab with which Bose became closely associated at a later stage. That very year, Jatindra Nath Das, a member of Bose's Congress Volunteer Corps, an accused in the Lahore Conspiracy Case, died in prison following a 64-day fast, demanding better treatment for revolutionary prisoners. Bose was deeply moved by the young man's self-

Bhagat Singh

sacrifice. He took charge of the funeral rites and when a series of youth conferences were organised in the different provinces of India, Bose presided over these meetings. The next year in April 1930, the Chittagong Armoury Raid Case seriously undermined the confidence of the British Government, when Chittagong's armoury was attacked by a band of young revolutionaries led by Surya Sen. The men seized all the weapons and slipped into the forested hillside to launch a guerilla warfare completely disrupting British rule in the region. Most of these young men had some association with Bose's Bengal Volunteer Corps.

While these sporadic, daring revolutionary activities continued to stun the British Raj, Mahatma Gandhi launched the second phase of his Non-violent agitation—the Civil Disobedience Movement (1930-34) that demonstrated to the world how non-violence could be used to arouse a whole nation and defy the might of an imperial power. Gandhi undertook a historic 385 km long march from Ahmedabad to Dandi, to make salt and break the Salt Law peacefully. When the report of the Simon Commission was published in June 1930, the Civil Disobedience Movement was in full swing. This would be followed by the three Round Table Conferences in London. Gandhi attended the second one in 1931, after briefly suspending the Movement following the Gandhi–Irwin Pact, which seemingly met with his demand for the release of political prisoners. However, Bose was disillusioned with the Pact as it failed to address the issue of release of the revolutionaries who had been imprisoned. And soon the other nationalist leaders also saw that they had very little to gain from the Round Table Conference. Gandhi now re-launched the Civil Disobedience Movement. Thousands of men and women, young and the aged, were lathi-charged and arrested, and the press gagged. Top nationalist leaders were all imprisoned, including Bose and later his brother, Sarat as well.

Bose had been critical of the idea of a Round Table Conference. Earlier he had stated, 'Mine is a programme of all-round boycott . . . ' for he believed that 'a round table conference is a conference between two belligerent parties . . . I ask you whether the people of India are invited to send any of their representatives with full powers to negotiate with the representatives

Gandhiji and Pandit Madan Mohan Malaviya at the Second Round Table Conference, 1931

of the British Government?' Bose, who believed in 'total boycott', emphasised that the workers, the peasants and the depressed classes of the country need to be well-organised for civil disobedience to succeed fully.

When Gandhi had launched the Civil Disobedience Movement, Bose was in prison. He had been arrested in 1930 while trying to implement his 'militant' programme and sentenced to a year's rigorous imprisonment. And in the very same year, while still in prison, he was elected the Mayor of Calcutta, a position earlier held by C R Das. Shortly after his release, Bose was severely beaten up for defying a ban. Once again, he was packed off to prison.

In August 1932, when the British government announced the Communal Award, giving separate electorates to different religious groups, including B R Ambedkar's demand for reservation for Harijans, Bose was still in prison. In response to the Communal Award, Gandhi undertook a fast unto death against the measure that aimed to create divisions among Indians, while Bose, as Sisir Kumar Bose writes, 'felt strongly that the British Government had this time definitely got the better of the Congress.' It was Bose's belief that 'until the radical or revolutionary elements are stirred up, we cannot get freedom', and he found the Congress lacking in this revolutionary radicalism.

Bose, 1932

As Bose's health began to suffer in prison, he was eventually released in February 1933 and put on a ship bound for Europe to his treatment for tuberculosis. On reaching Vienna, Bose, between 1933-36, began to

Bose as Mayor of Calcutta demonstrating on Independence Day, 26 January, 1931

champion the cause of India's freedom in Europe and when Gandhi withdrew the Civil Disobedience Movement in 1933, Bose, and Vithalbhai Patel, who was also in Vienna, issued a joint statement regretting the decision. During his sojourn in Europe, Bose also established contact with eminent European personalities like Mussolini; Romain Rolland, the French scholar; de Valera, the Irish leader and others. And he set up the Austria–India Society in Vienna and took a leading part in the formation of the Czechoslovak–Indian Association.

Towards the end of 1934, Bose returned briefly to India to see his ailing father. But by the time he reached Calcutta, where he was virtually kept under house arrest, his father had passed away. Early in January 1935, Bose returned to Europe for his treatment where he also published his book *The Indian Struggle*, which was critical of many Indian nationalists. The book, which was banned in India, was widely reviewed in the British press. Also in 1935, he underwent surgery for the removal of the gall bladder.

When the Government of India Act of 1935 was passed, the British government failed to give Indians a representative government and instead aimed to make India a federation of provinces. Nehru, the Congress Socialists, and the Communists were all violently opposed to supporting the

Act in any shape or form. Bose, then in Europe, also opposed the Act in toto.

In 1936, Bose returned to India, but he was soon arrested in Bombay. Eventually, he was transferred to Kurseong near Darjeeling, and detained at his brother's bungalow. Towards the end of the year, he was sent to Calcutta and admitted to the Calcutta Medical College on account of his health. Finally, he was released a year later in 1937, the year before he was elected the Congress President. But as Bose had not yet recovered completely, he decided to spend a few months in Dalhousie, the north Indian hill station, as a guest of the Dharamvirs, whom he had known for long, and then made a brief visit to Europe.

Bose with his wife Emilie, 1936

On reaching Naples, Bose took a train to Badgastein in Austria, where as he said, 'this combination of snow, sun, and dry cold . . . makes Switzerland and the west of Austria such a healthy place in winter. I had found just the weather I needed and the scenery I loved, and I was glad.' And there was another very good reason for his gladness—Emilie Schenkl, a Viennese lady, whom he had known since 1934, joined him here. Here, in about ten days, Bose wrote his unfinished autobiography *An Indian Pilgrim*, which covered the narrative of his life starting with his family background to childhood and education, to his youth and his decision to withdraw his appointment to the ICS in 1921. It was during this trip that Bose is said to have married Emilie Schenkl, whom he saw for the last time in 1943. They would live together in Berlin from 1941 to 1943 during his sojourn in Germany. Anita, their daughter, was born on 29 November 1942.

Bose returned to India in January 1936, when he was elected the Congress President. In a telegram, Gandhi had written to him saying, 'God give you strength to bear the weight of Jawaharlal's mantle.' When Bose arrived at the site of the Congress village of Haripura, for which the artist Nandalal Bose painted panels depicting scenes from everyday life, Bose was given a warm reception. Villagers garlanded and cheered him on his way as he passed by. According to a report, 'He received a most cordial welcome from the rural folk of Gujarat. Seated in an ancient *rath* driven by 51 lusty bulls of Gujarat, he was taken in procession', while bands played music and thousands greeted him all the way. Bose was the second Congress President elected from Bengal after Deshbandhu Chittaranjan Das, elected President at the Gaya session in 1922.

At the Haripura Congress, Bose's aim was to consolidate the socialist-leftist elements within the party into one bloc. He stressed the need for developing international contacts and 'an independent foreign policy', which he believed should not be influenced by the form or politics of the foreign state. He also stressed the need for friendly relations with neighbouring countries. He said, 'our chief national problems relating to the eradication of poverty, illiteracy and disease and to scientific production and distribution can be effectively tackled only along socialistic lines. The very first thing which our future national government will have to do would be to set up a Commission for drawing up a comprehensive plan of reconstruction . . .'

At Congress sessions as well as at other gatherings, Bose spoke incessantly for a new, vibrant form of Indian socialism. Like Nehru, he was an ardent supporter of socialism. 'The principles which should form the basis of our collective life are: justice, equality, freedom, discipline . . .'

he stated and '. . . in order to ensure equality, we must get rid of bondage of every kind—social, economic and political. . . .' His vision of freeing India of her bondage was based on the following programmes:

- Organisation of peasants and workers under a socialist programme
- Organisation of youth into volunteer corps under strict discipline
- Abolition of the caste system and the eradication of social and religious superstitions
- Organisation of women's associations
- Intensive programme of boycott of British goods
- Creation of literature for propagating the new programme

Bose realised early on that the 'first problem to tackle is that of our increasing population.' Another idea that he had advocated was the use of a blend of Hindi and Urdu, written in the Roman script, to be used as a common language. Since his visit to Turkey in 1934, he came to believe 'what a great advantage it was to have the same script as the rest of the world.'

Towards the end of his first term as President, a rift occurred between Bose and the Gandhian right-wing Congressmen over issues including inner-party democracy. Bose believed that the Congress cabinet should represent all the major points of view within the party. Gandhi on the contrary believed that it should represent members with one point of view. Bose, who believed that the Congress President should be elected on the basis of policies and programmes, was keen to stand for re-election as the Congress President for a second term. But Pattabhi Sitaramayya, supported by Mahatma Gandhi, was put up as the right-wing candidate as their nominee for the Congress President for the year 1939. But Bose, who wished to strengthen the left base through this election, won the contest successfully and Gandhi stated that Sitaramayya's defeat was his own defeat.

In 1939, Bose went to meet Gandhi at his Ashram in Wardha and when he returned to Calcutta, he became seriously ill. Nonetheless, he attended the Congress session held in March at Tripuri near Jubbulpore in Madhya Pradesh and his brother, Sarat Bose, read out the address. Gandhi, who was busy with the affairs of the princely state of Rajkot, however, did not come to Tripuri, where the conflict between Bose and the Gandhians came to a head. It revolved round what is called the 'Pant Resolution', initiated by Govind Ballabh Pant, a Gandhian. The resolution was passed by the members of the Working Committee, a majority of whom then resigned. The resolution called on the President, 'to nominate the Working Committee in accordance with the wishes of Gandhiji.' And it also demanded 'firm adherence to the fundamental policies' of the Congress under the guidance of Mahatma Gandhi.

The support of the Congress Socialists had led to Bose's re-election as the Congress President defeating Gandhi's candidate, but 'Congressmen did not see it as a rejection of Gandhi's leadership.' Now, the Pant Resolution clearly asked Congressmen to follow the Gandhian path. And the resolution, writes Nanda, '. . . clipped Bose's wings by reducing the issue at the Tripuri Congress to a vote of confidence in the Mahatma's leadership. This strategy at once robbed Bose of the support of the Congress Socialists, who had tilted the balance in his favour in the election.'

Though Gandhi freed Bose from the resolution and gave him the liberty to form a team of his choice, Bose realised that though he had won the election a second time, without the support of the Gandhians, it would not be smooth sailing for him. Finally, he resigned and Rajendra Prasad was elected to finish the presidential term. Comments Nanda, 'The year begun triumphantly for him with his victory in the presidential election but ended disastrously with his expulsion from the Congress. Bose himself claimed that he had been a victim of a political vendetta by the "Gandhiaites". But he knew he had provoked a crisis in the party.'

The international situation at this time was tense, with war clouds looming large on the horizon of Europe. The Second World War was imminent. Bose believed that this was 'an opportune moment' for intensifying the National Movement for independence and for launching a mass struggle to seize power from the imperial British. Writes Nanda, 'He believed that the British could be expelled from India with a mass upsurge—a final struggle—and that a golden opportunity for this struggle would arise when Great Britain became involved in a European War.'

With the Mahatma

Gandhi had by now begun to speak of the fundamental differences in principle between him and Bose. He stated, 'I think he still holds the view he had expressed at Jalpaiguri . . . It includes giving an ultimatum to the Government. He holds that we possess enough resources for a fight. Today, the whole atmosphere is so steeped in violence that I cannot think of fighting . . . This is a great and fundamental difference of opinion.'

Nehru too, whom Bose once looked upon 'as politically an elder brother', and often sought his advice, held a different ideological stance just as Gandhi did. Gordon writes that Nehru wrote to Bose, saying, 'The fact that in international affairs you held different views from mine and did not wholly approve our condemnation of Nazi Germany or Fascist Italy added to my discomfort.'

And Bose replied, again as Gordon notes in his book, 'It is no use championing lost causes all the time and it is no use condemning countries like Germany and Italy on the one hand and on the other, giving a certificate of good conduct to British and French Imperialism. . . . I have been urging . . . everybody . . . including Mahatma Gandhi and you, that we must utilise the international situation to India's advantage and . . . present the British Government with our National Demand in the form of an ultimatum; but I could make no impression on you or on Mahatmaji, though a large section of the Indian public approved of my stand.'

Soon after his resignation as the second-term Congress President, Bose announced on 3 May 1939, the formation of Forward Bloc, a new group 'within the Congress.' He also started the weekly journal *Forward* in order to, as he said, 'rally all radical and anti-imperialist progressive elements in the country on the basis of a minimum programme.' as well as press forward for freedom by a mass upsurge and a final struggle. The first all-India conference of

Congress Working Committee meeting at the Bose house, Calcutta, 1938

the Forward Bloc was held in Bombay in June 1939. In July, demonstrations were held throughout India demanding the right of all Congressmen to criticise and publicly discuss Congress policies. When Bose was asked not to hold these demonstrations, he went ahead nonetheless, with what he believed was his democratic right. Finally, the Working Committee debarred him from membership of any elective Congress Committee for three years from August 1939.

Meanwhile, the Second World War broke out in Europe in September 1939. And though Bose had fared through rough weather in his relationship with his party members, he was 'still an important figure in Congress', and he was invited to the special Working Committee meeting at Wardha from 10-14 September 1940, to discuss Congress policy on the war. Bose as usual spoke with his characteristic passion, reiterating that, 'A Britain at war meant a weak Britain . . . now was the time to launch the final struggle for independence with a great new Non-cooperation Movement.'

This argument of Bose and his socialist allies, write Read and Fisher in *The Proudest Day* '. . . was a powerful one. But there were many others who were enjoying power for the first time in their lives, and they were not eager to give it up.' Bose also vehemently resisted the idea of India's involvement in an imperialist war and stepped up the campaign against cooperation with the imperialists by organising huge public demonstrations in different parts of the country. An Anti-Imperialist Conference was held at Nagpur in October 1939. In March 1940, a massive demonstration was held at Ramgarh in Bihar, called the All-India Anti-Compromise Conference, at which Bose said, 'The age of Imperialism is drawing to a close and the era of freedom, democracy and socialism looms ahead of us.' And in June 1940, he organised a second conference of the Forward Bloc in Nagpur.

On 2 July 1940, Bose was arrested once again under the Defence of India Rules and imprisoned at Presidency Jail in Calcutta. This was his eleventh and last imprisonment for his activities against the Raj. However, on 5 December, he was sent home after he went on a fast-unto-death for ten days, protesting against his illegal detention.

Bose returned home to begin a bold new chapter in his life.

'Azad Hind'

Chapter Three

Between Two Escapes and After

In July 1940, when Bose was lodged at Presidency Jail in Calcutta, it is said, he probably made up his mind to escape from India and seek the assistance of Britain's international enemy, Germany.

So, soon after his release from jail in December 1940 and on reaching his residence at Elgin Road, Calcutta, Bose drew up an escape plan with nephew Sisir, his brother Sarat's son, and Mian Akbar Shah, a close associate and a Forward Bloc leader from Peshawar. According to the plan, Bose announced to his family members that he was going on a retreat for spiritual contemplation and no one would be allowed to disturb his privacy. Even his food was served in front of a curtain and he ate his meals in seclusion.

On 16 January 1941, Sisir arrived in his German Wanderer and once the city went to sleep, he drove off with Bose, evading the watchful eyes of a ring of spies and the police who kept

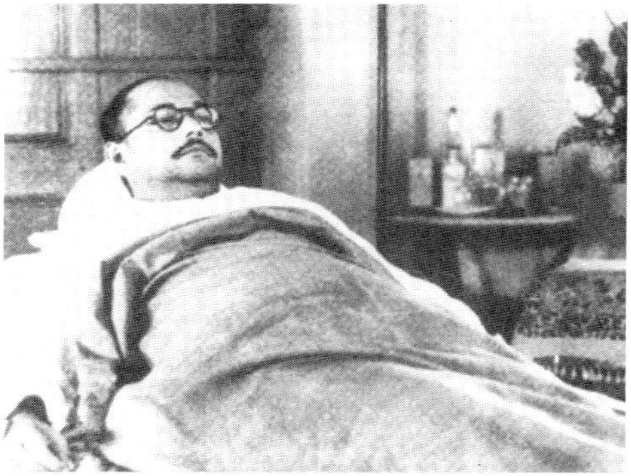

(left) Bose in his house before his escape, December 1940
(right) Bose after his release from prison with his mother, brother and the Mayor of Calcutta, AR Siddiqui, December 1940

constant watch on him. Next morning, the two arrived at the house of Sarat's eldest son, Ashoke, at Berari, a few miles from Dhanbad. Posing as an inspector of an insurance company, Bose travelled under the assumed name of Mohammad Ziauddin. After spending a night at Berari, the family dropped him at Gomoh. Here, Bose took the Delhi-Kalka Mail at midnight, reaching Peshawar on 19 January 1941, where he was received by Akbar Shah. Later, Bose moved from his hotel to one Abad Khan's house, where he stayed for six days disguised as a Pathan. Eventually, accompanied by Bhagat Ram Talwar, they left for the border of Afridi tribal territory in a car and then trekking across treacherous snow covered mountains, reached Jalalabad on 28 January. On 31 January 1941, the two reached Kabul by a *tonga* with Bose posing as Bhagat Ram's deaf and dumb brother. They claimed to be on their way to a shrine and ultimately to Kabul, where he was being taken for treatment.

Writes Sisir Kumar Bose, 'In Kabul, both of them were complete strangers. They looked for a serai. . . . The place was scarcely fit for human habitation. . . . For food, they had bread dipped in sweet tea. Although Subhas Chandra was out of the direct clutches of the British police, he soon discovered that his ordeal had only begun and not ended. For the next forty-five days, living in the most inhospitable surroundings and always in fear of being spotted by Afghan police or British agents, Subhas Chandra had the most trying time.'

In Kabul, Bose later shifted to the house of one Uttam Chand Malhotra, a businessman. Finally, after what seemed like an endless wait, he got in touch with the German Legation and then the Italian minister Alberto Quaroni. It was finally arranged that Bose would travel to Russia on an Italian passport, impersonating as Orlando Mazzotta, an officer of the Italian Legation in Kabul. On 18 March, Bose left in a car for the Soviet frontier accompanied by three Germans. Finally, he reached Samarkand and then travelled by rail to Moscow. Here, he took a flight to Berlin, reaching his destination on 2 April 1941, more than two months after he made his dramatic escape from Calcutta.

In Berlin, Bose was received by the German Foreign Office and shortly afterwards he presented a comprehensive memorandum—a set of proposals—for winning the goal of Indian Independence. The memorandum called for the setting up of:

- A Free India Government in exile in Berlin, to be recognised by Germany and run with the help of a loan that was to be paid back later (which he later partly paid off from South-East Asia)
- A Free India broadcasting centre to encourage Indians to stand up for their freedom and stir a revolt against the British
- A military force of 50,000, organised and trained in Germany to drive out the British from India

Bose also called for an agreement between Germany, Italy, and the Free India Government, declaring Indian independence after an Axis victory in the Second World War.

Bose's proposal however, did not meet with the level of enthusiasm that Bose had hoped for. Writes Rudolf Hartog in his book *The Sign of the Tiger: Subhas Chandra Bose and His Indian Legion in Germany, 1941-45*, 'On the one hand, Bose was completely ignored and rejected by the leaders and the Nazi Party. On the other hand, the Foreign Office and the German High Command spared no pains to support him. It was the Foreign Office which recognised him as the leader of a provisional free Indian government with the title of "Excellency" and a diplomatic residence in Berlin's Lichtenstein Allee 10. It was the German Army Command (OKH) which provided the means to set up and train a regiment of Indian volunteers.'

'The main incentive came from the Foreign Office, in particular from Dr Adam von Trott zu Solz and his colleagues Dr Alexander Werth and F J Furtwangler, who supported him personally and coordinated the extensive propaganda broadcasts to India over the strongest short-wave station available.'

While in Germany, Bose devoted considerable time to bringing together a group of Indian students living there and in other European countries. On 2 November 1941, the Free India Centre was established with members like M R Vyas, N G Swami, N G Ganpulay, C Nambiar, Abid Hasan, Girija Mookerji and others. The activities of the Centre included broadcasts over the Azad Hind Radio; publication of the bi-lingual periodical *Azad Hind* (German and English), which appeared from early 1942; and coordination with Bose's German-trained military force that he was trying to organise. The radio broadcast was made by 'a powerful German transmitter located at Huizen in Holland and Podiebrad in Czechoslovakia' and made in seven languages (English and Hindustani plus Bengali, Tamil, Telugu, Gujarati and Pushtu). The first transmission made on 6 January 1942 is said to have cost one million Reichmark. The Free India Centre also

Bose talking to war prisoners who agreed to join the Indian Legion

set up a Planning Commission for social and economical reorganisation of India after attaining independence. The Centre had its own insignia—it was the Congress tricolour with the outline of a springing tiger embossed on it and the poet Rabindranath Tagore's *Jana-gana-mana* was adopted as the national anthem.

Bose, as mentioned earlier, had always been keen on having a military wing organised for the Indian National Movement. He had said, 'Throughout my life it was my ambition to equip an army that will capture freedom from the enemy.' This wish finally resulted in the formation of the Indian Legion and later in the Azad Hind Fauj in South-East Asia. On 19 December 1941, the Germans officially agreed to train Indian war prisoners who volunteered to join Bose's military force—the Indian Legion. Germany and Italy agreed that Italy would hand over the captured Indian prisoners of the British army to the Germans, and they would be transported in batches through 1942 to Camp Annaburg, near Dresden for training. The Indian Legion, thus formed, was an entirely volunteer army consisting of all communities—and all religions—Hindus, Sikhs, Muslims, Punjabis, Marathis and Bengalis—yet, it never got a role to perform during the struggle.

It was not until after almost a year's wait that Bose finally met Hitler briefly on 27 May 1942. But a declaration supporting Indian independence that he had wanted from the Germans did not come through. Quoting from the minutes of the interview with Hitler by his chief interpreter P O Schmidt, dated 30 May 1942, Rudolf Hartog notes in his book that instead, Hitler advised Bose, 'to go to the Japanese, who were closer to the Indian frontier. He also advised Bose to avoid the journey back by air as he was, "too important a person to risk his life," and offered to find him a safe passage back either by a Japanese submarine which was at the moment in Europe, or he said, he would put a submarine at his disposal to take him to Bangkok. He then "showed the route over the Cape of Good Hope on the map and estimated that the journey would take six weeks." '

Bose and his Indian Legion at the oath-taking ceremony, Germany

As Hartog writes, the meeting was 'not a success for Bose and it ended for him on a note of frustration.' Earlier too, the German invasion of the Soviet Union on 22 June 1941 had been most disappointing for Bose—like an 'almost physical blow'. Leonard A Gordon writes in his book *Brothers Against the Raj* that Dr Woermann, of the Political Section in Berlin, is said to have noted that when Bose met him he had stated that, 'in India they believed that the Soviet Union was an anti-imperialist power and thus the natural ally of India against England . . . In the German-Russian war the feelings of the Indian people were very decidedly on the Russian side, because the Indian people were sure that Germany was the aggressor and thus also an imperialist power dangerous to India.'

Netaji in Rome, Italy, with a German air force officer

However, in spite of his many disappointments, Bose carried on with the activities of his Centre while in Germany. In February 1942, after the Japanese overran Singapore, Bose himself started broadcasting to India. 'The hour of India's salvation is at hand. India will now rise and break the chains of servitude that have bound her so long,' he stated with firm conviction.

Early in 1943, a German-Italian plan was in place for Bose to undertake yet another dramatic and daring underwater sea voyage by submarine to South-east Asia. Accompanied only by one companion, Abid Hasan, Bose reached the North German port of Kiel on 8 February 1943. Here Keppler, the German Secretary of State in the Foreign Office, and Nambiar and Werth came to see off Bose, who left by the German submarine U-18, commanded by Commander Werner Musenberg. At the initial stage, Bose's vehicle was protected by a convoy of submarines and a minesweeper. His underwater sea voyage took him through the waters around the British Isles and the Atlantic Ocean full of enemy ships, and round the Cape of Good Hope to the Indian Ocean. Inside the submarine for three months, everything stank of diesel oil, including the food. And as Hasan, Bose's companion wrote, 'I was quite

(above) 'Free India'
The insignia of the Indian Legion worn as a flash on the right sleeve of the uniform. The background is in the national colours of India and the springing tiger is the symbol of the fight for freedom

(below) Oath-taking ceremony, July 1942. Gurmukh Singh is holding the 'Azad Hind' flag

On the German Submarine with Captain Musenberg, 1943

fascinated by the romance of having to travel by a submarine. But the moment I entered the submarine, all romance of it went away.'

On 24 April 1943, the German submarine met with the Japanese submarine I-29 commanded by Juichi Izu in the Mozambique Channel, east of Madagascar. Writes Sisir Bose, '. . . the sea was too rough and it was impossible to get the two boats near to each other. Radio conversation was too risky. As a desperate measure, two men jumped into the sea from the German submarine and swam to the Japanese. . . . Eventually, the two Germans rode a rubber raft dragging a strong hemp rope back to their boat. Bose and Hasan crossed over in the rubber raft clinging to the rope and inching their way amid surging waves and lurking sharks. The transfer was effected . . . and a radio message flashed to Berlin.'

In Tokyo, 1943

The Imperial Japanese Navy was now in charge of Bose's journey ahead and from here, the Japanese submarine reached Saban Island, an islet north of Sumatra. After a few days of rest, Bose reached Tokyo by air on 13 May 1943.

On 10 June 1943, Bose met the Japanese prime minister Tojo, after waiting for three weeks. Tojo was so impressed by the Indian leader that he met him again after four days. Two days later, on 16 June 1943, Bose was invited to the Diet, the Japanese Parliament, where Tojo declared, 'We are indignant about the fact that India is still under the ruthless suppression of Britain' and expressed his total sympathy with India's 'desperate struggle for independence'.

Issue of stamps for Bose's National Government, Berlin 1943-44

'Azad Hind'

Chapter Four

The Indian National Army

An Indian independence movement had been underway in South-east Asia prior to Bose's arrival in Tokyo. Following the outbreak of the Second World War, the Japanese began to make friendly overtures to the one-and-a-half million strong Indian community in South-east Asia. They had gauged that the defense of British territories in the region largely depended on the loyalty and the strength of the British Indian army stationed there. It was therefore, in Japan's interest to sabotage this loyalty. In pursuance of this policy, Major Fujiwara Iwaichi, a Japanese intelligence officer, was assigned the task of making contacts with the Indians in Thailand and the Indian troops defending Malaya and Singapore.

In March 1942, a General Conference of the Indian Movement was called in Tokyo with Japanese support in the name of Rashbehari Bose, the veteran Indian nationalist, who had been living in exile in Japan for the past quarter of a century. Meanwhile, Colonel Iwakuro replaced Fujiwara in taking charge of the Indian affairs. On 15 June 1942, a large gathering of Indians took place in Bangkok, 'to formally merge the diverse Indian organisations in South-east Asia into the Indian Independence League (IIL).' As the idea of a formation of an Indian liberation army had been earlier floated by a Sikh, Gianni Pritam Singh, and Fujiwara, the IIL now sanctioned the formation of the Indian National Army (INA) under Captain Mohan Singh, an Indian officer of the British army who had walked over to the Japanese side. Henceforth, the INA was formed by enlisting the voluntary services of thousands of Indian army prisoners captured by the Japanese when they marched through Malaya and Singapore. The executive body of the IIL, the Council of Action, under Rashbehari as the President, put up the following demands:

- That the INA be accorded the status of an allied army on equal footing with the Japanese
- That Indian national independence and India's absolute sovereignty be recognised
- That the Japanese Government should help in bringing over Subhas Chandra Bose to the East

Mohan Singh had popularised the belief among Indians living in the region that Indians would rise up against British imperialism, if 'a revolutionary like Bose could be persuaded to come to Asia to lead the Movement.' The news of Bose's work in Berlin had spread to the East. Writes Gordon, 'an idealised image of him was passing into the minds of South-east Asian Indians.' This was described by Fujiwara as a great admiration for Bose, 'amounting almost to a religious devotion.'

On 1 September 1942, the First Division of the INA, numbering 16,300 men, came into existence, and by the end of 1942, 'forty thousand men expressed their willingness to join the INA.' But there was a general mistrust of the Japanese commitment to Indian nationalism and as there were, 'numerous incidents of Japanese arrogance', Indians felt that the Japanese intention was primarily 'to use the INA for their own narrow objectives.'

Eventually, by the end of 1942, Mohan Singh fell out with the Japanese over the role of the INA. Another member was arrested and the INA disbanded. But a couple of months later, the Indian army was once again reorganised under Colonel Bhonsle, who had under him Lt Col Shah Nawaz Khan as Chief of General Staff, Major P K Sahgal as Military Secretary, Major Habibur Rahman as Commander of the Officers' Training School, and Lt Col A C Chatterji.

With Bose's arrival in Tokyo, six months later, the Indian Independence Movement gained a new momentum as much as it did from the Quit India Movement, then sweeping through India, when on 8 August 1942 the Congress passed a resolution asking the British to quit India. Gandhi called upon his countrymen to, 'do or die' and declared, 'We shall either free India or die in the attempt.' The Japanese too were now keen to have Bose in the East. After their victory in Malaya and Singapore in February 1942, followed by gains in Burma, the Allied forces had begun to inflict losses on the Axis. And as Bose was getting ready for his journey to the East in early 1943, the Germans suffered their greatest defeat at Stalingrad.

On 2 July 1943, Bose moved to Singapore, where he was given a hero's welcome and profusely garlanded as he took over charge of the Indian Independence League from the elderly Rashbehari. He now became the supreme commander of the INA or the Azad Hind Fauj, which he began to reorganise and for which funds were collected.

Addressing his soldiers here for the first time, Bose said, 'Throughout my public career, I have always felt that, though India is otherwise ripe for independence in every way, she has lacked one thing, namely, an army of liberation. George Washington of America could fight and win freedom, because he had his army. Garibaldi could liberate Italy because he had his armed volunteers behind him. It is your privilege and honour to be the first to come forward and organise India's national army. By doing so you have removed the last obstacle in our path to freedom . . . Comrades! My soldiers! Let your battle-cry be "To Delhi! To Delhi". How many of us will individually survive this war of freedom, I do not know. But I do know this, that we shall ultimately win and our task will not end until our surviving heroes hold the victory parade on another graveyard of the British Empire—Lal Kila or the Red Fortress of ancient Delhi . . .'

Bose now set up a Provisional Government of Azad Hind or Free India on 21 October 1943, which was recognised by nine States—Japan, Germany, Italy, Croatia, Manchukuo, Nanking, the Philippines, Thailand and Burma. He took charge of his government as the Prime Minister and was also the minister in charge of war and foreign affairs, and his government declared war on Britain and America. And on 22 October 1943, against Japanese discouragement, Bose inaugurated a women's brigade of the Azad Hind Fauj—the Rani of Jhansi Regiment, named after Rani Laxmibai, the sole woman to lead her soldiers against the British in the Great Uprising of 1857.

Bose attended the Assembly of Greater East Asiatic Nations as an observer in Tokyo in November 1943, when he called for a new world order committed to justice, national sovereignty and cooperation among nations. And before leaving for Singapore in December, he toured China, the Philippines and Indonesia.

After the Japanese occupation of the Andaman and Nicobar islands, Prime

Minister Tojo had announced that the occupied islands would be handed over to the Provisional Government of Azad Hind. On 24 December 1943, Bose was handed over the islands as the first free territory of his government—though critics say it was only in name—and the national flag hoisted. The Andaman and Nicobar Islands were named Shahid and Swaraj Islands.

By the beginning of 1944, Bose moved his headquarters to Rangoon, which was closer to the Indian frontier, as the Japanese prepared to launch the Imphal campaign by moving through the Indo-Burmese border into Manipur and northeast India. Though the INA had asked for a significant role in the war and talked of equality between the two armies, the Japanese military officers are said to have often rebuffed such an idea, assigning the Indian soldiers only secondary roles like building and repairing roads. Besides, the Japanese were not in a position to adequately equip the INA with weapons, food and other supplies. However, one division of the Indian National Army commanded by Shah Nawaz accompanied the Japanese army and succeeded in entering Kohima and then in reaching within ten miles of Imphal by the end of April. It was here that Bose made his famous speech:

'There, there in the distance, beyond that river, beyond those jungles, beyond those hills, lies the Promised Land—the soil from which we sprang and the land to which we shall now return. . . . We shall carve our way through the enemy's ranks or, if God wills, we shall die a martyr's death. And in our last sleep we shall kiss the road that will bring our army to Delhi. The road to Delhi is the road to Freedom! *Chalo* Delhi!'

On 6 July 1944, Bose broadcast over Azad Hind Radio an address to Gandhi saying, 'Whatever I have done has been for the benefit of my nation . . . Father of our nation! In this holy war for India's liberation we ask for your blessings and good wishes.'

However, by the end of 1944, the war situation began to change in favour of the Allied army of Britain and America and the fall of Rangoon became imminent. The Japanese had begun to retreat by the middle of 1944 and by mid-1945, the tables were turned in the war game. As they evacuated from the city, Bose was asked to join them. But he refused to retreat without the Rani of Jhansi Regiment and through a most difficult and dangerous terrain, through rain and floods, they returned to Bangkok after a month. Writes Sisir Bose, 'Vehicles in Bose's convoy broke down one by one. He had, therefore, to march miles and miles in the company of brave women soldiers . . .'

Bose visiting the Cellular Jail at Port Blair, Andaman Islands, December 1943

On 14 August 1945, when the Japanese made an unconditional surrender to the Allied powers, Bose was in Singapore, but he held his head high, stating, 'The roads to Delhi are many and Delhi still remains our goal.' And he began to draw up a plan to move into the Soviet territory from where he wished to continue with the Indian freedom struggle. But first, it was decided Bose would return to Tokyo. Accordingly, on 15 August 1945, accompanied by Habib-ur Rahman, Abid Hasan and others, Bose left by plane for Tokyo. On the way the plane halted at Saigon, where he was put on a Japanese bomber accompanied by Habib-ur Rahman, as there was only one extra seat available. After leaving Saigon, they spent the night in Tourane in north Indo-China. On 18 August, they flew to Taiwan. On 23 August 1945, Tokyo Radio announced that the plane in which Bose was

Bose's official welcome at Rangoon airport by Burmese leaders led by Ba Maw, 1944

travelling had crashed while taking off from Taihoku airport. Bose passed away the same night at the military hospital, having sustained severe burn injuries.

After the end of the Second World War, when news spread across India of the maltreatment of the INA prisoners by the British Government and its intention to put these men on trial, Nehru reacted sharply stating that, 'the punishment given to them would in effect be a punishment on all India and all Indians.' And the Congress promptly set up a defence committee headed by Bhulabhai Desai for the trial of the three INA officers, Shah Nawaz, P K Sahgal and G S Dhillon.

Bose's grand scheme of uniting the nationalist movement abroad with that in India into a massive struggle to oust the British from India ended in a fiasco, just as the Great Uprising of 1857 had. But were Bose's endeavours and his struggle all in vain? The INA trial had an 'electrifying' effect on the people of India, and Bose and the INA now 'became household names,' throughout the country as the returning soldiers were sought to be prosecuted by the British Government. And as Michael Edwards rightly noted, that though the British Government had hoped that the prosecution of the INA members would help to reinforce the morale of

Bose inspects the women's regiment of the INA – the Rani of Jhansi Regiment, 1943

the Indian army, it instead, succeeded only 'in creating unease, in making the soldiers feel slightly ashamed that they themselves had supported the British . . . if these men who were being defended had been on the right side, as all India now claimed, then the Indians in the Indian army were on the wrong side . . . It slowly dawned upon the Government of India that the backbone of the British rule, the Indian army, might now no longer be trustworthy. The ghost of Subhas, like Hamlet's father, walked the battlements of the Red Fort (where the INA soldiers were tried) and his suddenly amplified figure overawed the Conference that was to lead to independence.'

In the war cemetery at Kohima, where the INA had reached, in spite of all its weaknesses and against all odds, the following lines are tellingly inscribed on a plaque:

'When you go home, tell them of us. For their Tomorrow we gave our Today.'

'Azad Hind'

Chapter Five

Heir to a Life Immortal

After interviewing Subhas Chandra Bose at his Berlin residence, Luigi Barzini, an Italian journalist, whom Gordon quotes in his book *Brothers Against the Raj*, gave a pen-portrait of the man in the following words:

'He is young, tall . . . with a kind of smiling expression, high forehead, finely drawn mouth, altogether a feeling of superior intelligence . . . The composure and control of himself . . . constitute . . . a sign of Asiatic nobility . . . He was a faithful and active follower of Gandhi, and still speaks with devotion and admiration of the Mahatma, but he has become in certain respects his antagonist.'

One of the most eloquent tributes ever paid to Bose was by the poet laureate, Rabindranath Tagore, who, though he said had 'misgivings' in his heart at an earlier time, stood by Bose in his troubled days when he was re-elected as the Congress President and soon thereafter when he resigned. Tagore gave him a warm reception at Santiniketan in January 1939 despite the controversy that surrounded him at that time, and when he heard of his resignation, he wrote to Bose saying, 'The dignity and forbearance which you have shown in the midst of a most aggravating situation has won my admiration and confidence in your leadership.' And in an essay *Deshanayak* (The Country's Leader) Tagore penned:

'As Bengal's poet, I today acknowledge you as the honoured leader of the people of Bengal . . . Today you are revealed in the pure light of the midday sun . . . You did not regard apparent defeat as final: therefore, you have turned your trials into your allies . . .' And he continued, 'I am addressing at this meeting one who has come into the full light of recognition . . . I may not join him in the fight that is to come. I can only bless him . . . knowing that he had made his country's burden of sorrow his own . . .'

Bose narrates an incident from his life in his *An Unfinished Autobiography* that left a deep impress on his mind, 'I sometimes wonder how at a particular psychological moment a small incident can exert a far-reaching influence on our life. In front of our house in Calcutta, an old, decrepit beggar woman used to sit every day and beg for alms. Every time I went out or came in, I could not help seeing her. Her sorrowful countenance and her tattered clothes pained me whenever I looked at her or even thought of her. By contrast, I appeared to be so well off and comfortable that I used to feel like a criminal. What right had I—I used to think—to be so fortunate to live in a three-storeyed house when this miserable beggar woman had hardly a roof over her head and practically no food or clothing? . . . Thoughts like these made me rebel against the existing social system.'

Resolute, assertive and ever 'irrepressible', as Gandhi found him to be, Bose, right from his youth—the time he left home in search of a guru and his decision to withdraw from the ICS—to the very end of his life, displayed a rare dogged determination in following his convictions. Writing to Sarat, while at Cambridge, he had recalled, 'Looking back on my school days, I have no doubt that I must have appeared to others as wayward, eccentric and obstinate . . . nothing mattered to me except my inner dreams, and the more resistance I met, the more obstinate I became.'

That was Bose. There was a streak of the rebel in him from a very early age. But what shaped his life, in his own words, were 'two things forced me to develop politically and to strike out an independent line for myself . . . the behaviour of Britishers in Calcutta and the Great War.'

By temperament Bose was drawn to risks, challenges and struggles for as he wrote, 'Life loses half its interest if there is no struggle—if there are no risks to be taken.' And behind all his actions his 'principles' ever guided him. Writing to the Government while he was in Presidency Jail in 1940 when he had decided to go on a hunger strike, he stated, 'What greater solace can there be than the feeling that one has lived and died for a principle? . . . What higher consummation can life attain than peaceful self-immolation at the altar of one's cause.'

That Bose was different from others—and in some respects ahead of his times—was quite obvious to him. He wrote, '. . . I had in some respect a touch of the abnormal in my mental make-up. Not only was I too much of an introvert, but I was in some respects precocious. The result was that at an age when I should have been tiring myself out on the football field, I was brooding over problems which should rather have been left to a more mature age.'

When Bose was rusticated from Calcutta University for his alleged assault on Professor Oaten of Presidency College, he was described as, 'the most troublesome man'. The British Government too, soon discovered that this indeed was the case—'he was too dangerous to let loose,' and that it was safer to keep him behind bars or have him shipped to Europe on forced exile on the grounds of his ill-health which required specialised treatment. Ever since his imprisonment in Mandalay, his health had begun to suffer. As Gordon explains, 'He had digestive problems and recurring pains around the waist. He was put on a liquid diet diet of Horlicks and chicken soup but continued to lose weight. The cause of his symptoms was unclear and gall bladder trouble and tuberculosis were suggested.' And as Tagore wrote in his tribute to Bose, 'Your strength has been sorely taxed by imprisonment, banishment and disease, but rather than impairing, these have helped to broaden your sympathies.'

A satisfied Bose, the Indian Legion had been formed, April 1942

Yet, in spite of his ill-health, Bose among all the Congressmen of his time was more frequently jailed and kept under detention. On 10 May 1936, Jawaharlal Nehru, then the Congress President, called for an All-India Subhas Day to protest against his prolonged detention. And in 1940, Bose himself went on a hunger strike to protest against his unlawful detention.

'Fiery and distinctly un-Gandhian,' as Bose has been described, he often became embroiled in controversies, particularly after his re-election as the Congress President followed by his subsequent resignation, and later when he escaped to Germany to seek help in India's freedom struggle from Hitler, the man responsible for one of the worst genocides committed against humanity. Jawaharlal Nehru, 'a steadfast anti-fascist' had strongly opposed his courting of the Germans, saying, 'Hitler and Japan must go to hell. . . . Mr Bose acted very wrongly, though in good faith.' Again, Nehru had stated, 'I do not . . . doubt the bonafides of Mr Bose. I think he has come to a certain conclusion, which I think is wrong, but nevertheless, a conclusion which he thinks is for the good of India. But I do realise that the way he has chosen is utterly wrong.'

Mahatma Gandhi too, whose non-violent politics showed 'sharp differences' with that of Bose, was opposed to the idea of 'bringing in foreigners in order to help us win our liberty,' which Gandhi feared could end in 'exchanging one form of slavery for another, possibly much worse.' There was thus, a fundamental difference between the policies of Bose, Nehru and

Bose with Col. Satoshi Yamamoto, military attaché of the Japanese embassy in Berlin. Members of the staff of the Free India Centre are standing behind them, Königsbrück, 1942

Subhas Bose with Indira and Jawaharlal Nehru, 1938

Gandhi. For, while Gandhi was ideologically opposed to the use of any violence in politics, Bose believed in the politics of opportunity, and as Machiavelli would have approved, in the ultimate goal. His argument was '. . . it is no use condemning countries like Germany and Italy on the one hand and on the other, giving a certificate of good conduct to British and French Imperialism . . . we must utilise the international situation to India's advantage and . . . present the British government with our National Demand in the form of an ultimatum.'

Did Bose subscribe to fascism while attempting to win the support of Hitler's Germany? Rudolf Hartog in *The Sign of the Tiger* says that Bose denied such a charge after his return from a trip to Europe in an article in the *Amrit Bazaar Patrika*, dated 11 January 1935. Bose wrote, '. . . as far as his principles are concerned, I do not see how they can appeal to India . .

. . I earnestly deplore the tendency to reproduce in India the fascist and communist systems blindly.'

Throughout his life, Bose remained close to his brother, Sarat, and his wife, Biva, who showered unconditional love and affection on him and gave their constant support through most difficult of times. And like his brother Sarat, a Congressman and a patriot who went in and out of jails, Bose staunchly believed in a secular, united India, which could never be divided along communal lines. He passionately believed in a free and an egalitarian, socialist India, where there would be 'complete religious and cultural freedom for individuals and groups' with no 'state religion.' In this he was like Gandhi, who too had fondly recalled the memory of Bose, when the partition of India became a fact. As Read and Fisher note in their book *The Proudest Day,* 'At least,' he (Gandhi) said, 'Bose had shown in his organisation of the INA how Hindus and Muslims could work together in a great cause.'

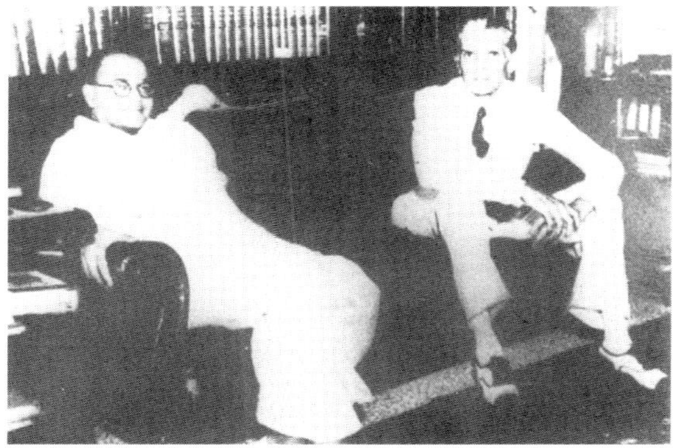

Bose with Jinnah, 1938

Bose pursued his own ideology single-mindedly and though he had become alienated from the Congress mainstream from 1939, he had a large following among the youth, particularly in Bengal. Here, a Subhas Congress Fund was started when Bose wanted to have an office for the Bengal Congress, which was to be a centre for nation-building activities. For this, the Calcutta Corporation gave a piece of land for a small fee. And Tagore, in spite of his poor health, travelled from Santiniketan to lay the foundation of this Congress building in August 1939, which he named Mahajati Sadan. Read and Fisher state, 'He was such a hero to the Bengalis that, as Ian Stephen, editor of the *Calcutta Statesman* observed, he would only have to parachute on to the maidan beside the Hoogly river in Calcutta, and 90 per cent of the population would rise up and follow him.' This was in fact, Bose's belief that once the INA successfully established a hold on Indian soil, the entire country would rise and join his revolutionary thrust into India, but that was not to be, as his dream was cut short at Imphal.

As it is said, nothing succeeds as success. And failures win no accolades. Bose's 'shortsightedness' in working with the Axis resulted in a fiasco. B R Nanda notes, 'While Bose was second to none in his patriotism and self-sacrifice, he seems to have been deficient in political judgment . . . His grand plan for liberating India with the help of the Axis powers was ill-conceived and did not work out as he had visualised; he discovered to his dismay that in the war strategies of the Fascist leaders of Germany and Japan, India's freedom was the lowest priority.' But undoubtedly, as B R Nanda adds, 'Among India's nationalist leaders in the inter-war years, Jawaharlal Nehru and Subhas Bose were, after the Mahatma, the most charismatic figures.' Bose's self-sacrifice at the alter of his country, his commitment to the cause of India's freedom, and his devotion to his beloved motherland were indeed, rare and extraordinary.

'Nobody could lose through suffering and sacrifice. If he does lose anything of the earth, he will gain more in return by becoming the heir to a life immortal,' Bose believed. He sacrificed his life for India's freedom and though he did not live to see India become a free nation, he is indeed, the heir to a 'life immortal.'

'Azad Hind'

JAI HIND

SUPREME COMMANDER,

AZAD HIND FAUJ.

The last available photograph of Netaji – 17 August 1945

THE ENIGMA OVER SUBHAS CHANDRA BOSE'S DEATH . . .

CITY THROBS

FOR A PERMANENT PEACE

&

PEOPLES' DEMOCRACY

NETAJI IS ALIVE

American Sources Confirm

NETAJI !!

The Nation Pays

Homage To You

ডাক

THE CALL

নেহেরুর শব-পার্শ্বে

কে এই সন্ন্যাসী ?

For years a controversy raged over the official report of Bose's death in a plane crash. Plain devotion or a mystery?
'Netaji is Alive American Sources Confirm', Front page of Calcutta weekly, 1965

Sadhu resembling Subhas Bose viewing Jawaharlal Nehru's body, 1964.
From Dak, *a Bengali weekly. 'Who is this sannyasi?' the editors ask*

Cartoon showing Subhas Bose driving off Churchill – from Menga Mainichi, *a Japanese cartoon daily, January 1945*

CHRONOLOGY

1897 23 January, birth in Cuttack, Orissa.

1902 Joined Protestant European School, Cuttack.

1909 Joined Ravenshaw Collegiate School, Cuttack.

1913 Stood second in the Matriculation Examination; joined Presidency College, Calcutta.

1914 Passed Intermediate Examination in first division. Gandhi arrived in India from S. Africa.

1916 Debarred from studying further at the University for misbehaviour with a British professor at Presidency College; left for Cuttack.

1917 Returned to Calcutta; re-admitted to Scottish Church College with honours in Philosophy; Gandhi began his Satyagraha at Champaran.

1919 Took his BA degree with first class honours; sailed for England in September to take the prestigious ICS examination; Massacre at Jallianwalla Bagh.

1920 Passed the ICS examination in London with highest marks in English and came fourth in the merit list; Gandhi launched the Non-cooperation Movement.

1921 Resigned from his ICS appointment; returned to India in July; met Gandhi in Bombay and C R Das in Calcutta; began to work for the weekly *Banglar Katha* and took part in various nationalist activities; formed the South Calcutta Sevak Samity; in December both Bose and Das imprisoned for eight months for anti-British activities.

1922 Bose in prison, when Gandhi withdrew the Non-cooperation Movement; released from jail in August; worked for *Atma Sakti*; joined the Swaraj Party formed by Motilal Nehru and Das at the Gaya Congress.

1923 Elected President of All Bengal Youth League; elected General Secretary of Bengal Provincial Congress Committee; became the editor of the English language daily *Forward,* founded by Das.

1924 The Swarajists won the Calcutta Municipal elections; Das elected the first Mayor of Calcutta; Bose appointed the Chief Executive Officer; arrested again in October and sent to jail in Mandalay for three years

1925 Bose still in prison; C R Das passed away.

1926 Elected to the Bengal Congress while still in prison.

1927 Elected General Secretary of the All India Congress Committee; Simon Commission set up by Lord Irwin.

1928 Took charge of the Bengal Volunteer Corps at the Calcutta Summit of the Indian Congress and was elected General Officer in Command; Bose called for 'complete Independence' at the Calcutta Congress, instead of 'dominion status'.

1929 The Indian nationalist movement took a revolutionary turn; Gandhi called for *Purna Swaraj*; Tricolour flag unfurled; at the Lahore Congress, Bose called for 'parallel government' of India.

1930 Arrested in January and sentenced to a year's rigorous imprisonment while trying to implement his 'militant' programme; elected Mayor of Calcutta while in jail; report of the Simon Commission published in June; the Civil Disobedience Movement (1930–34) launched by Gandhi. First Round Table Conference.

1931 Elected President of All India Trade Union Congress; shortly after his release, severely beaten up for defying a ban and taken into custody; Gandhi attended the Second Round Table Conference in London and returned to re-launch the Civil Disobedience Movement.

1932 At the Karachi Congress under the Presidentship of Vallabhbhai Patel and at the second session of the Nawjawan Bharat Sabha, Bose called for a new, vibrant form of Indian socialism and advocated a socialist order for free India.

1933 Left for Europe in February on forced exile. Reached Vienna in March, where he was under medical treatment; between 1933–1936, met reputed personalities in Europe like Mussolini; met Vithalbhai Patel, and after Gandhi withdrew the Civil Disobedience Movement, Bose and Patel made a joint statement of disapproval.

1934 Received news of his father's illness and left for India. Kept under house arrest at his residence in Calcutta for a month.

1935 Returned to Europe in January for medical treatment. During this period of exile, wrote his book *The Indian Struggle*, published in London in January. The Act of 1935 passed.

1936 Returned to India in April briefly; arrested again in Bombay. Eventually, transferred to Kurseong and detained at his brother's bungalow; removed to Calcutta, admitted to the Calcutta Medical College; in May an all-India hartal was observed to protest against his continuous detention.

1937 Released from detention in March; shortly visited Europe—Badgastein in Austria, where he married Emilie Schenkl; in about ten days, wrote his book *An Indian Pilgrim: An Unfinished Autobiography.*

1938 Returned to India in January; elected Congress President at the Haripura Congress; as President wished to consolidate the socialist–leftist elements within the party into one bloc; formed the National Planning Commission.

1939 Re-elected Congress President after defeating Gandhi's candidate Pattabhi Sitaramayya; felicitated at Santiniketan by Rabindranath Tagore; the Pant Resolution passed at the Tripuri Congress session; resigned as Congress President and formed the Forward Bloc; Congress Working Committee debarred him from membership of any elective Congress committee in August; held Anti-imperialist Conference at Nagpur in October.

1940 Held a massive demonstration at Ramgarh in Bihar in March, called the All-India Anti-Compromise Conference; in June organised a second conference of the Forward Bloc in Nagpur. On 2 July, arrested under the Defence of India Rules and imprisoned at Presidency Jail in Calcutta, his eleventh and last imprisonment; on 5 December, sent home after he went on a fast-unto-death for 10 days.

1941 On 16 January, escaped from his Elgin Road residence; reached Peshawar on 19 January and Kabul on 31 January. On 18 March, left for the Soviet frontier and after reaching Samarkand, travelled by rail to Moscow. On 2 April, reached Berlin by air. Submitted a Memorandum to the German government—an outline plan of cooperation with the Axis powers; met Hitler in Berlin; on 2 November, set up the Free India Centre; on 19 December, German approval for the training of Indian war prisoners who agreed to join his military force, the Indian Legion.

1942 On 6 January, first radio transmission from Azad Hind Radio; publication of periodical *Azad Hind*; formed the Indian Legion; in February, the Japanese overran Singapore and he himself started broadcasting to India; in March, a General Conference of the Indian Movement in Tokyo called with Japanese support; on 15 June, a large gathering of Indian troops in Bangkok formally merged the diverse Indian organisations in South-east Asia into the Indian Independence League that sanctioned the development of the Indian National Army (INA) under Mohan Singh.

1943 On 8 February, started for Japan by submarine; on May 13, reached Tokyo; on 10 June, Bose met the Japanese Prime Minister Tojo; delivered a speech on Tokyo Radio; on 2 July, he moved to Singapore and convened a meeting of the Indian Independence League; on 21 October, formed the Provisional Government of the Azad Hind or Free India and on 22 October, inaugurated the Rani of Jhansi Regiment; visited the Andaman Islands in December.

1944 In January, moved his headquarters to Rangoon; the Azad Hind Fauj and the Japanese forces entered Burma; the Imphal Campaign and Azad Hind took control of Kohima, reaching within miles of Imphal; the Allied powers brought in reinforcement, thereby changing the tide of war; by the end of the year fall of Rangoon imminent, his army retreated; addressed a massive public meeting in Kuala Lumpur.

1945 Delivered a speech on air from Sonam radio; Hiroshima and Nagasaki destroyed by atom bomb; on 14 August, Japan surrendered; on 15 August, left for Tokyo to work on future plans; on 23 August, he passed away following a plane crash in Taiwan.

BIBLIOGRAPHY

Bose, Sisir Kumar: *Netaji Subhas Chandra Bose*, National Book Trust, India, 1986.

De, Sailesh: *Ami Subhas Bolchhi* (Bengali), Bishwabapi Prakashani, Kolkata.

Gordon, Leonard A: *Brothers Against the Raj: A Biography of Indian Nationalists Sarat and Subhas Chandra Bose,* Columbia University Press, New York, 1990.

Hartog, Rudolf: *Subhas Chandra Bose and his Indian Legion in Germany, 1941–45,* Rupa & Co, New Delhi, 2001.

Nanda, B R: *The Making of a Nation*, HarperCollins, India, 1998.

Read, Anthony and David Fisher: *The Proudest Day: India's Long Road to Independence*, Jonathan Cape, London, 1997.

Subhas Chandra Bose: *An Indian Pilgrim: An Unfinished Autobiography*, edited by Sisir K Bose and Sugata Bose, Oxford University Press and Netaji Research Bureau, 1997.

ACKNOWLEDGEMENT

I am grateful to the expert authors listed above for the data I have used from their valuable books.

AUTHOR'S PROFILE

Reeta Dutta Gupta worked as a freelance journalist from the late 1970s to the early 1990s, and contributed articles, reviews and interviews to the *Times of India*, the *Hindustan Times* and other national papers. She lived in Africa for several years and her first children's stories set in Africa appeared in two anthologies: *The Nose Doctor* and *The Best of Target Stories*. The titles of her children's books are *Grandmother's Tales, Midnight Train and Other Ghost Stories, How Mnjini Became a Magician and Other African Tales*, and a short picture book *Monuments of India*.

Her other books include short biographies, *Rabindranath Tagore: The Poet Sublime*, and *Salim Ali: India's Birdman*, and a work of fiction, *I Am Radha*.